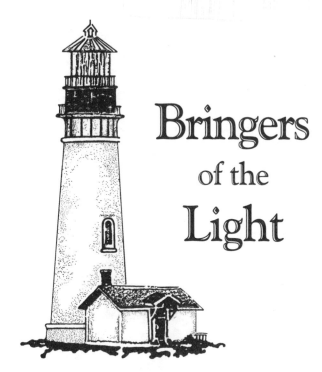

Bringers
of the
Light

By Neale Donald Walsch

Author of *Conversations with God*

Published by
Millennium Legacies Inc.
PMB #1144
1257 Siskiyou Blvd.
Ashland, OR 97520

Distributed by
Hampton Roads Publishing Company
1125 Stoney Ridge Road
Charlottesville, VA 22902
call: 1-800-766-8009
email: hrpc@hrpub.com
web site: http://www.hrpub.com

If you are unable to order this book from your local
bookseller, you may order directly from the distributor
above. Quantity discounts for organizations are available.

Library of Congress Catalog Card Number: 00 091352
ISBN 0-9678755-0-1
Printed in Canada
10 9 8 7 6 5 4 3 2

In memory of

Francis H. Treon

a Futzu (Master) in Gohn Dagow

(a classical, southern Chinese, soft,

monk form of self development),

who devoted his life to being a

Bringer of the Light.

The world needs your Light now.

Not tomorrow. Now.

Of course, you know this. That's why you've found your way to this book.

This book will tell you how to shine your Light. It's a very simple book, about a very simple process. Yet the process, though simple, may not seem easy. So listen. Watch. Pay attention.

Listen to what this book has to say. Watch the results in your life. And pay attention to how it's all falling together.

It is falling together, you know. It may not *look* like it, but it is. Usually when your life looks like it's falling apart, it's really falling together. Often, for the first time.

There's a reason for that. It has to do with a very sound metaphysical principle. Briefly stated:

As soon as you decide Who and What You Are, everything unlike it will come into the space.

Life has no choice but to show up this way, and so you can expect it as sure as you're reading this.

It is important to understand this principle if you are going to be a *Bringer of the Light.* It is a principle you *must* understand, or you cannot hope to undertake this work.

However, before exploring this principle, you should be thanked. You should be thanked for being the kind of person who would want to read this book. You don't know how much that means to the world right now.

Unless you do.

There's a lot of pain out there. There's a lot of darkness. The world needs your Light right now.

It really does.

So...glad you could show up. Now the fun starts. Now the challenge gets underway in earnest. Now the healing begins.

With you as the Healer.

That's what you're here for, as if you didn't know. That's why you came to the Earth, in this body, in this time and in this place.

A Course in Miracles puts it very directly:

> *You are in the room to heal the room.*
> *You are in the space to heal the space.*
> *There is no other reason for you to be here.*

All the information in this book falls into one of two categories: **Principles** and **Steps**. There are five of each. That is, **Five Steps** toward becoming a *Bringer of the Light*, and **Five Principles** which may be used to better guide those steps.

One of these Principles has just been stated. It will be necessary to understand *each* of the Five Principles in order to take the Steps necessary to be what you now declare that you wish to be.

This book will be woven like a tapestry, with the Principles intertwined into a text describing the Steps, so that you will clearly see the relationship between the two.

Bringers Step 1

Get clear about the purpose of your life.

L et us look, then, at the first Step in your process of becoming a *Bringer of the Light*

If you're like most people, you may not have given Life Purpose much thought in your earlier years. As a result, you may have spent a great deal of time doing things which at the end of your life will not matter; will mean nothing. Not to you, not to anyone. What you really have to do if you want to get on the fast track of evolution is to put each golden moment of Life to its highest and best use. You cannot know what that is unless and until you decide on a

Purpose. That is, you cannot decide *how* to get where you are going until you decide *where* you are going.

One day a man stopped his car at the corner of a friendly street in a friendly town and motioned to a friendly person standing nearby.

"Excuse me," the driver said, "but I seem to be lost. Could you kindly give me directions?"

"Certainly, sir," said the person on the street. "Where are you trying to go?"

"I don't know," the driver answered.

"Well, sir," said the person who was trying to help him, "You must first tell me where you want to go before I can tell you how to get there."

If your life is directionless, it is because you have not *set* a direction. If your life is without accomplishment, it is because you do not know what you are seeking to accomplish. If your life has seemed pointless, it is because you have not sought to use it as a tool with which to *make* a point.

Which brings us to **Principle #1: Life is pointless.**

Principle #1

Life is pointless... and that is God's Greatest Gift.

This may come as a shock to many of you who think that there *is* a point to life, and that it is our job to find it, to uncover it, to learn it, to unravel it, to somehow, someday, somewhere discover it — and then live up to it.

It may come as a shock also to many others of you who think that you have *already* discovered the Point of Life, and *are* living up to it. (Most people who fall into this category haven't really "discovered" the Point of Life, they've been *told* what the Point of Life is, and they've accepted that.)

Yet there *is* no Point to it all. Life has no point. If Life had a Point, who would assign it one? And if you say God, why would God create the Point, then make us all search for it for 50 years? (And, as a society, for 50 *thousand* years.) And if you say God does not make us search, but has given us the answer, why did God not give us the answer in a way in which we could easily understand it, and with a formula upon which we could all agree? And if you say that God has done *that*, then you have not looked at the world lately.

No, God has not done that. And the reason God has not told us what the Point of Life is, is that there *is* no Point to Life. Life is pointless.

And that is God's greatest gift.

Think about it.

It is precisely because God has not emblazoned His purpose across the pages of Life that Life itself is an Open Book. A book that *we* get to write. We get to decide what purpose *we* choose.

If God had chosen a purpose — if God had a purpose designed into the plan — would God not tell us what that purpose was? Would God allow us to spend years, decades, *centuries*, searching, searching, searching for the point of it all?

Again, it must be said to those of you who are now thinking, "But God *did* announce the purpose of life!": if that is so, God did a pretty bad job of it, because if you look around you, you will see that *no one got it*.

Okay, a few. A few think they have gotten it. They

know the purpose of life, and it's just all the rest of the people who don't understand.

Well, that, of course, is the stance taken by *many of the Earth's major religions!* These religions teach that they know the purpose of life. There is even a religion or two which says it *is* the purpose of life, and that all we have to do is follow the dictates of that particular religion and we will have pleased God mightily — and be saved.

On the other hand, if we do not follow the dictates of that particular religion, we will be sent to the everlasting fires of hell.

None of this would be such a problem if it weren't for the fact that there are hundreds of organized religions making essentially the same claim.

Could God have really botched the job this badly? If God really established a purpose for Life, and really wanted us to know what that was, do you suppose this is the best God could do when it comes to communicating that to us in a way we could all understand?

Or is it possible that the reason we can't seem to agree on the point of it all is that there simply *is* no point?

In fact, that is exactly the case. Yet this may be difficult to accept for many people until it becomes clear *why* there is no point.

There is no point because God wants *us* to *create* a purpose for our life. And if God had already created that purpose, He would have robbed us of the greatest opportunity, and the greatest tool, that we have as we seek to perform the *function* of life.

Because, you see, while Life does not have a purpose, it *does* have a *function.*

Purpose and *function* are not at all the same thing. A clock *functions* by ticking, for the *purpose* of telling time. A car *functions* by internal combustion, for the *purpose* of moving people from place to place. A microwave oven *functions* by causing food molecules to vibrate very fast, for the *purpose* of heating food.

Life *functions* in a particular way, but for no predetermined *purpose.* That's because God created as the function of Life the *determining* of a purpose. Put another way:

> *Your function
> is to create the
> point of your life.
> In so doing, you create Your Self.
> You decide
> who and what you really are —
> and who you are going to be.*

God, you see, is in the constant process of creating and recreating Itself anew. God is in each moment deciding what God *is going to be next.* This is God's most exciting function. (In fact, it is God's *only* function.) This is pure creation.

(For a better, and complete, understanding of this Truth, see *Conversations with God - Book One* (Putnam Publishing Company, New York City, NY).

This principle is presented here so that you may understand that God has not *assigned* a purpose or a point to your life. God is waiting for *you* to do that. It is *you* who must create a *raison d'etre.* And that is what you have not yet done. You have not created a *reason for being.*

So **Step 1** here is *to decide and to declare* what life is all about — for you. What is the purpose of your life? If you can't answer that question, go to a larger one: What is the Purpose of Life in general?

Now... and here's the tricky part... *do not look anywhere else for an answer.* Just sit down and *decide this for yourself.* Don't ask yourself... *tell* yourself!

Tell yourself the purpose of Life in General, and then tell yourself what *your* purpose in life is going to be.

Now your first reaction to this suggestion may very likely be a feeling of "overwhelm"... as in "I'm on *overwhelm.*"

You may think that the subject is just too big; that the topic is outside the sphere of your understanding. It is not. And you will see that it is not the moment you give yourself permission to truly start thinking about this.

Truly start thinking about the real purpose of life and all *sorts* of ideas will begin to come to you. They will crowd in on you so fast, you won't know what hit you. Soon, if you stay with the process, you'll start discriminating. That is, your mind will start throwing out the absurd ideas and will quickly find itself left with only a few good ones. And just as soon as it reduces the list to those few, it will reduce the list even further. Left to your own devices, you will come up with what you think the purpose of life might be before you know it.

That is to say, you will know it before you *know it.*

In truth, there is a great deal that you know that you do not *know* that you know. You are carrying around knowledge you do not know that you have. Or, to put this another way, *you don't know the half of what you know.*

The only way to find out what you know is to *call upon yourself to know it.*

That is a mouthful right there, and you may want to go over that statement again.

'The only way to find out what you know is to call upon yourself to know it.'

The problem will not be in your not knowing the

purpose of Life, the problem will be in your *believing* that you know it.

In other words, it will be easier deciding for yourself what the purpose of Life is than it will be to agree with yourself that your answer could be correct!

The reason for this is that you still think that there *is* a "correct answer" — and if there is, you couldn't possibly have just guessed it!

Yet there is no "correct answer!"

The function of your life is to *give the question an answer* — and the answer that you give to the question *is* the "correct answer."

Yes... God has given you that much authority.

Yes...God has given you that much freedom.

Yes...God has given you that much power to create.

You do not believe this, and so you have spent years trying to figure *out* the Purpose of Life. And all the while, Life (God) has been waiting for you to *decide* Its purpose.

For now, don't try to understand this whole process, or the why's and wherefore's of it. For now, just follow instructions. It'll all become more clear to you later. This book is about how to become a *Bringer of the Light*. It is not about explaining the metaphysics of the entire universe. Because of its limited scope, this book requires that you take some statements on faith and simply follow instructions.

The instruction is:
Get clear about the purpose of your life.

So do that now. Right now, write out the Purpose of your Life.

Make a Statement of Purpose.

As suggested earlier, if you have to start with a larger statement, do so. Complete the following sentence:

The purpose of life in general is...

_____

_____

_____

Then complete a second sentence:

The purpose of My Life is...

_____

_____

_____

Have you done that? Good. Now you can go on.

What? Not finished yet? Stuck? Can't seem to do it? Re-read *Conversations with God.* Take notes this time. Then, re-read the first pages of this book. Take more notes if you have to. Look deeply at what you don't seem to understand. Or, if you have understanding, but just can't seem to bring yourself to do it, look deeply at what you cannot allow yourself to do.

This is a process in itself, which will be very valuable to you.

When you feel you can clearly state the purpose of life in general, and the purpose of your life in particular, move on.

Translate your purpose from Doingness to Beingness.

Some of you may have already done this – or may have *started* with a statement of Beingness. If you have, go right to Step 3.

For those of you who have not made this translation, or don't even know what is being talked about here, read on.

To be a *Bringer of the Light* one must understand the difference between "doing," and "being," and between "doingness" and "beingness."

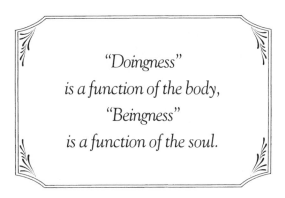

"Doingness"
is a function of the body,
"Beingness"
is a function of the soul.

Right Livelihood is seldom attained through a doingness decision . . . although it may *involve* a doingness *function* somewhere along the way.

Right Livelihood is easily attained through a beingness decision . . . which leads to a doingness function somewhere along the way.

To move into Right Livelihood, one must decide what one wishes to BE, not what one wishes to DO. Doingness must spring from Beingness, not the other way around.

To understand the difference between these two life experiences, explore **Principle #2.**

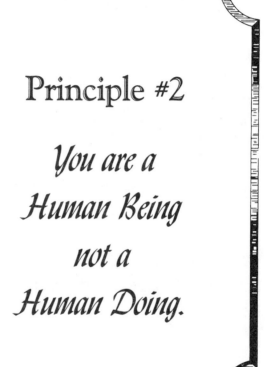

Principle #2

*You are a
Human Being
not a
Human Doing.*

I t is true that every minute of your life your body is doing something. Yet it is doing something for a reason. Everything you have willfully caused your body to do, you have caused it to do because there is some state of being you wish to achieve . . . and you *know no other way to achieve it.*

Think about this a minute.

Your body goes through the motions of eating – you cause it to eat; you make it "do" that – because you want it to be nourished. You are seeking to be the thing called *healthy.*

You sleep because you are trying to be the thing called *rested* – which you know leads to the same thing as above . . . namely, healthy.

You sit because you are trying to be the thing called *comfortable.* You stand because you are trying to more of the thing called *mobile.* You talk because you are trying to be the thing called *understood.* You listen because you are trying to be the thing called *understanding.*

The list goes on and on, but it never changes. Always it points through the thing called Doing, to a thing called Being.

Everything you willfully cause your body to do, it does in order to assist you in achieving a state of *Being.*

Do the following exercise. In the chart, make a list of things your body has done recently, then indicate the *Beingness* you were seeking to achieve.

We've started the list for you, to give you an example of how to complete the entries.

This is an excellent exercise to help you define and clarify the motives behind all of your actions.

Doingness	Beingness I wish to achieve
Reading this Book	*Wisdom, clarity, understanding*
Writing the author	*Sharing, connecting, expressing*
	Fill this in yourself
Cleaning the dishes	

Now it is true that there are some things your body does which you do not willfully cause it to do. When your body does one of these things, it is doing it *automatically,* not willfully. The body's *automatic* responses are reflections or announcements of a State of Beingness which has already been attained, rather than attempts to attain one.

Did you follow that? Are you clear about this? Let's look at some examples.

When you laugh, that is an *automatic* response to a State of Beingness which has already been attained, called *happy, joyful* — or, in some cases, *nervous.*

When you cry, that is an automatic response to a State of Beingness which has already been attained, called *sad, sorrowful* — or, in some cases, *happy.*

When your heart rate increases wildly, that is an automatic response to a State of Beingness which has already been attained, called *excited* — or, in some cases, *scared.*

When your heart rate decreases, producing a slow and steady pulse, that is an automatic response to a

State of Beingness which has already been attained, called *peaceful, serene.*

So we see that Automatic Doingness Functions of the body are used by the mind to reflect *a Beingness State, while Willful Doingness Functions are used by the mind to* achieve *a Beingness State.*

In both cases it is the mind which is causing the body, signaling the body, to "do" what it is "doing" — and it is the mind which thinks that "doingness" is the only way to achieve "beingness."

If you are still unclear about the *automatic* vs. *willful* paradigm, talk to any actor about it.

For an actor, being told to "laugh out loud," or to "begin to cry on that line," can be a nightmare ...unless the actor has learned to *be* the thing that *creates the automatic response* the director requires.

Yes, there are so-called "technical" actors who can produce the bodily action on command... but in more recent years it has been the "method" actors — actors such as Dustin Hoffman, Al Pacino, Meryl

Streep — who have gained the widest respect. Many say their acting seems somehow more "real." That is because they are not "acting like." They are *being.*

In "method acting" the actor *thinks of a thing,* or *remembers a time,* which produced the same emotional response in the past as the one now called for by the script. By this device the actor's mind tricks the body, causing it to cry, or to smile, or even to break into gales of laughter. When the mind sends the body a signal, the body doesn't know whether what the mind is experiencing is "real," or only a memory. To the body, it is all the same.

That is why the body's heart rate will increase, and the body itself may even break out in a cold sweat, at the memory of a beautiful woman, or a wonderful man, and a passionately romantic time. Nothing is happening in the present moment, but the *body doesn't know that.* It receives precisely the same signals from the brain as it did when the adventure was first experienced.

Fear can likewise be recreated with a memory,

which in turn produces bodily responses exactly as if the experience was occurring all over again.

To repeat, then: the mind can "tell" the body to "do" things for two different reasons. It can tell the body to "do" something in order to *achieve* a State of Being (this is called a Willful Action), or it can tell the body to "do" something in order to demonstrate the State of Being it has *already* achieved (this is called an Automatic Response).

In any event, you are always being something. And your body is always demonstrating what you are being. Sometimes the demonstration is very subtle, and sometimes it is not, but the demonstration never ends.

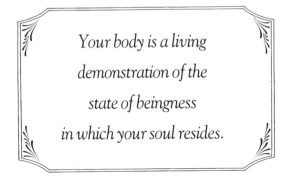

Your body is a living demonstration of the state of beingness in which your soul resides.

Returning now to **Step 2**, what you are asked to do is take a look at the declaration you came up with in **Step 1** when asked to declare your Life Purpose. Is the declaration a statement of "beingness" or a statement of "doingness"?

If it is a statement of "doingness," **Step 2** now asks you to *translate that into a Statement of Beingness.*

Use the chart on page 25 as a guide.

The reason you are asked to do this is that *only when your Doing flows out of your place of Being, announcing it rather than seeking to create it, can you ever be centered enough to become a Bringer of the Light.*

Most of the world has this "being/doing" paradigm backwards. People are running around everywhere doing, doing, doing, and hoping by this device to one day achieve a state of beingness ("happy," "peaceful," "abundant," "enlightened"...whatever) that will make it all worthwhile.

The sad thing about all this is that for most people, it doesn't work out that way. They spend their whole life doing this and doing that, doing this and doing that, and all they wind up with is a great big pile of "do-do."

So complete **Step 2** now, if you haven't already done so. Take any doingness statement which may have found itself into your declaration of Life Purpose and translate it into a beingness description.

Then...move on.

Bringers Step 3

Adopt right now
the state of being
you have described,
no matter what you are doing.

O kay, you've moved through the first two steps toward Right Livelihood and toward becoming a *Bringer of the Light*.

A person in "right livelihood," by the way, *is* a *Bringer of the Light.* That is because all people in right livelihood are *being who they really are*...and Who You Really Are is the *very Light you are seeking to bring!*

Did you get that? Did you hear that? There is no brighter Light in the Universe than the Light of your Beingness. Therefore, let your light so shine before men, that they may see your good works, and glorify your Father which is in heaven.

For He said unto them, "Is a candle brought to be put under a bushel, or under a bed, and not to be set on a candlestick? Neither do men light a candle, and put it under a bushel, but on a candlestick; and it giveth light unto all that are in the house."

Remember, you are in the room to heal the room. You are in the space to heal the space. You are in the house to heal the house... to "giveth light unto all that are in the house."

There is no other reason for you to be there.

How do you shine the Light of your Being? By first moving into Right Livelihood – which means by not allowing yourself to do anything for a living which violates your deepest inner sense of Who You Are.

You don't have to take any precipitous action in this regard however. For when you adopt and follow **Step 3** in the process which is being outlined here, you will find yourself *automatically* moving away from "wrong livelihood." It will happen in just the right way, at just the right time. You may even find that you have *caused yourself to be fired* from a job which you should never have had, or at which you should never have remained. This will all look like the boss' doing if you are not careful, and only when you have the most discerning eye will you be able to see that you brought it all on yourself (usually...even if subconsciously...quite deliberately).

So don't go out now and just quit your job. That's not what this book recommends, and that's not what this process is all about.

Yet do not be surprised if, as a result of the process of *moving towards Beingness* that you have undertaken, you discover a few weeks or months from now that you are no longer engaged in the work which currently fills your days.

It is in this moment that you will discover:

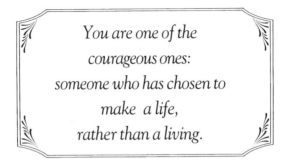

You are one of the courageous ones: someone who has chosen to make a life, rather than a living.

Step 3 often produces such a quantum shift in people's experience. That is because Step 3 is in itself a quantum movement. It is a movement from focus upon what you are *doing* to what you are *being*.

Let's try a little experiment in that focus shift right now. At this very moment, you are reading a book you are holding in your hand. That is what you are *doing*. If someone called you right now and said, "What'cha up to?" you'd say, "Oh, I'm just reading this neat little book." You'd answer that way because most of the time you are thinking about what you are *doing*. You look to see what your body is involved

in, and that is how you answer the question. It is
quite natural, given how you have focused your life.

But now, focus on what you are being. Right now,
this moment. What are you *being?* Close your eyes
and stay with the question.

Good. Now complete the following sentence:
Right now I am being...

_____

_____

_____

_____

Good. That's very good. You're getting the idea.
That clarity about what's going on with you comes
only when you focus on what you are being, right
here, right now.

Now, what we notice is that your present state of
Beingness may not seem to be one that you pre-

selected. That is, you may experience that the beingness you described in the completed sentence just above is a beingness which was *induced*, if you will, by your reading this book.

We often see our States of Being that way. We imagine them to be induced, or caused, by our exterior experience. Yet look now at **Principle #3.**

Principle #3

*Everything
you are being,
you are being because
you choose to be.*

If, at any given moment, you are being afraid, it is   because you choose to be. If you are being joyful, it is because you choose to be. If you are being annoyed, it is because you choose to be. If you are being harassed, it is because you choose to be.

If you are being loved, it is because you choose to be. If you are being ignored, it is because you choose to be. If you are being helped, it is because you choose to be. If you are being hurt, it is because you choose to be. If you are being wise, it is because you choose to be.

If you are feeling wronged, it is because you choose to be.

This list could go on forever.

Indeed...it actually does.

Understand that *beingness* is a State in which one *is*, not an action which one takes.

You cannot *do* "happy," you can only *be* "happy," depending upon what *you decide* to be.

You cannot *do* "sad." You cannot *do* "afraid." You cannot *do* "wronged," or "hurt," or "annoyed." You can only *be* these things.

And what causes you to *be* them? Many people believe it is what is going on around them; that it's what someone or something else is doing. Yet it is not. It is your *decision* about what someone else is doing which causes that. It is the *choice you make*.

The complexity surrounding this whole business is this: so many of the choices you are making are now so automatic, so deeply based in prior experience, that they seem to be noncontrollable by you. And so it *looks as if* the actions of others, or experiences exterior to you, are causing the response within you.

Yet the truth is, you are choosing to be in the State in which you find yourself. And the only difference between you and those who have mastered this life is that Masters choose differently.

(For a far more detailed exploration of this subject, see *Conversations with God - Book One*.)

The point to be made here is that *beingness* is chosen, not induced. You *chose* to be whatever you wrote on page 44. *Why* you chose it is another matter – the subject for another whole book. Yet this much we know: the choice was not forced. Choices may often *seem* forced, but they never are.

You *can* produce a State of Being by simply *selecting one*. And you can do this *anytime, anywhere*.

A State of Being is a feeling, not an action. Yet you can undertake to feel *a certain way*. That is, you have the power to *decide how you're going to feel*, and how you feel *right now*.

This is the great secret of the human encounter. This is the great gift, and the great tool. And with this tool all the Universe is opened unto you, and all the freedom you could ever want to be and to experience Who You Really Are is granted you.

This is the Truth; the Truth which shall set you free.

Y ou need to at least accept this Principle as a possibility in order to make it work. When you can accept it as a possibility, go back to **Step 3**. Choose to move into the State of Beingness you have described in **Step 2**, and choose to *be that*, no matter *what* you are "doing."

This is the formula through which people move into Right Livelihood. It is, to use the title from a wonderful book by Terry Cole-Whittaker, *The Inner Path from Where You Are to Where You Want to Be.*

So choose now that State of Beingness you wish to experience in, as, and through you. Then be that. How? It is a matter of focus. It has to do with what you focus your attention upon.

Let's try one State of Being, just for an example. Let's pick...*peacefulness.* Let us say, just for the purpose of this exercise, that you wish and choose to experience yourself in a State of Peacefulness at all times, everywhere.

Good. Now concentrate on that for a minute. Get in touch with that. See what that feels like. Put the book down, relax for just a minute, and go to that place right now.

Good. Now choose to *be* that...choose to *be peace*...every minute of every hour for the rest of this day. Do you think you can be that? You can if you *stick to your commitment.* Because if you stick to your commitment, and remain focused on your Purpose (to *be "peace"*), what you will find is that your body *automatically does things* to assist you and to allow you to *experience that beingness.*

One thing your body will do is bring you into contact with, or cause you to notice, everything unlike what you now choose. (Principle 4, in the next section, will explain why.) Then your body will *lead you to peace*, and lead you *away from* that which is not peaceful. It will no longer find it comfortable or possible to do otherwise, so will perform all manner of tricks.

It will move out of noisy rooms, for instance. And it will choose to forget about the evening news tonight on TV. It will suddenly find certain music unacceptable. It will even perform more subtle tricks. It may find a way to block out the traffic sounds on your drive home after a long day at work, or mute the normally ear-piercing shrieks of boisterous children in the back seat as you head to the supermarket. It may choose to ignore what could be otherwise oppressive heat, or to experience as "uneventful" the previously painful encounters at the dentist's office.

You have all learned about mind over matter in this way. You have all "forgotten" about a headache, or "ignored" a momentary frustration, in favor of a larger or more important experience you chose to have. This process we are calling **Step 3** is not different from that. *It is a process you have used over and over again in your life.* What is remarkable about it is not that you have used it before, but that you do not think you can use it *whenever you wish.*

Now, as stated earlier, the degree to which your body begins to automatically do things which allow you to remain in a State of Being depends on the degree of commitment and determination you demonstrate.

We have all seen how this process works in smaller ways in everyday life. If you are *determined* to "be" a thing — whether it's the thing called "peaceful" or the thing called "joyful" or the thing called "successful" — *nothing in the world can stop you.*

That is also true if you are determined to be the thing called "depressed," or "upset," or "unable," Nothing, *nothing,* in the world can stop you.

Ever try to enliven a person who is determined to be sad? You can just forget it. You're wasting your time.

The same is true of a person who is determined to be at peace.

So if you determine to "be" a certain thing (that is, to express, experience and fulfill a State of Beingness upon which you have decided), and if you *stick with your decision* no matter what the appearance of things, your body will sooner or later find itself *automatically doing things* which tend to enhance the possibility of producing that beingness in your experience.

Before long, your *mind* will also join the action. You are, after all, a three-part being — Body, Mind and Spirit — and all three aspects of your being will soon be engaged if you make, and stick with, a **Beingness Decision**. That is because Beingness Decisions are triggers which fire reactors in every fiber of your being, at every level of your functioning. They are the keys which start the engine of Creation.

This explains why, once a Beingness Decision is made, you will begin to automatically eliminate from your life everything unlike what you seek to be. This you will do on an almost subconscious level. That is to say, *you may not even be aware that you are doing it.* Your concerned family, friends and co-workers may even say, "Are you sure you know what you're doing?" You won't be able to answer them, because, in truth, you may *not* be sure.

You have allowed, in a sense, your automatic functions to take over. These include your instincts, your responses, your inner discernment. This is what happens when you "let go and let God." You may find yourself reaching for that cigarette, and then suddenly putting it down for no reason...never to pick one up again. Or calling some friends, and placing the receiver back on the hook, never to hang out with those people again. Or going to work, but turning around and coming back home, never to go back to that place again. Something inside of you will just tell you, "no more." Some intuitive messenger will simply say, very quietly, "It's time to quit. It's time to move on. It's time to change." And all the fear, all the anxiety you may have had around that will suddenly be gone.

So don't be surprised — if you stay *focused* on the State of Beingness you select — to find after a matter of days, weeks or months that you have simply eased out of certain friendships, and "gravitated" towards others; eased out of certain physical environments, and gravitated towards others; eased out, yes, even of your job, and gravitated toward other ways of "making a living." Sooner or later you will stop "making a living" altogether...and will spend all of your time *making a life.*

This is the movement which will take you towards Right Livelihood. This is the process by which you will create and express your True Self.

You will discover, if you trust this process, that you *can* adopt a State of Beingness (and more than one state if you wish), and move into the experience of that. And you will discover that your state of inner Being will, and should, have nothing to do with the state of your outer experience.

Dentist's chair or noisy kids in the car, none of it will make any difference. The exterior circumstances of your life will no longer control and create the interior experiences of your Soul.

You will easily and effortlessly move away from and eliminate those exterior conditions which you wish to eliminate, and hang on to those you wish to retain (regardless of how "disruptive" they used to be, for you will no longer find them "disruptive"), and thus *recreate yourself anew* in the image and likeness of Who You Really Are.

Still, there are some things you should know about this process you are being asked to trust.

Observe Opposition
and call it Opportunity.

The first thing you need to know is that there will be opposition. Opposition in the form of people, events and circumstances which will seem to create a barrier to everything you say you are; everything you declare yourself to *be*.

As a matter of fact, not only will there be opposition — but the opposition will *increase*. It will be greater than it ever was before. So if you thought you had problems before, hold onto your hat, because, in the words of the inimitable Jimmy Durante, "You ain't seen nuttin' yet."

(If you haven't the foggiest notion who Jimmy Durante is, move two spaces back and lose a turn;

do not pass GO, do not collect $200.)

The fact that "things are going to get worse before they get better" may not be the most exciting news you've heard since picking up this book. Still, you must be told — and when you understand why this is so, you will actually rejoice should things take a downward turn.

It all has to do with **Principle #4:**

Principle #4

As soon as you decide who and what you are, everything unlike it will come into the space.

T his is how it is, and this is how it *must be.* But now, try to understand why.

To grasp what you are about to be told, you have to see clearly the Truth about Opposites. The Truth about Opposites is that they *don't exist*, except *in the space of each other*.

That is to say, "hot" does not exist except in an environment or space in which there is "cold." "Tall" does not exist except in the space of that which is "short." "Fast" cannot even be a concept unless and until there is a thing called "slow."

In the World of the Relative (which is, by the way, the world in which you have chosen to spend most of your time), a thing is only what it IS relative to ANOTHER thing that it is NOT.

Do you understand? That may sound a bit confusing, but do you get it? You should hear that as an enormous Truth ringing in your ears.

It's just another way of saying that in our present state of existence, everything is relative.

Yet the principle, applied to metaphysics, yields

some very interesting insights. For if a thing is nothing except in the space of that which it is not, then YOU cannot be ANYTHING except in the space of that which YOU are not.

And so the opposite of what you wish to "be" will appear almost as soon as your wish to "be" it is heard. Indeed, your Soul draws these conditions to itself. And God will give the Soul everything it calls forth, as the Greatest Gift of the Grandest Creator, in order that the Soul may fulfill Itself in this, Its highest desire.

Thus will the Soul thank God for those treasures which are called the Conditions and Events of Life, and thus will the Soul welcome all of Life's experiences, honoring them equally, the "good" and the "bad," without judgment.

If you feel that you understand the concept embodied in this basic principle of life, go back now to what was said in **Step 4.**

We said, "Not only will there be opposition — but the opposition will *increase*. It will be greater than it ever was before." We also said, "when you under-stand why this is so, you will actually rejoice should things take a downward turn."

The reason you will rejoice is that you will know — for you will see "opposition" as a sure and certain sign — that you are on the journey of transforma-tion; the road to glory; the higher path.

It is now important for you to also know that in a *very real* metaphysical sense, there is "a light at the end of the tunnel." The appearance and the effect of these negative opposites we have talked about is but temporary, and their purpose is to heal forever *any* negative feeling you have had about the outer experiences of your life.

Here is how this healing occurs.

Let's use Peace once again as our example. Let's say that you are a parent, and you have made the declaration, "I am *Peace*." Now the moment you make that declaration, everything *unlike* "peace" will come into your experience. And so the kids will start making noise — more noise than ever before!

Yet now you will be at *choice* in responding to this, for now you will know and understand *why this is happening.* You may choose to see this "opposite" as a *gift bearer*, bringing you a chance to experience and express peace, or as a thief, stealing your peace *from* you.

Let's assume you choose to be peace. With this commitment and focus, you do not respond in the old way; you do not become just as noisy and chaotic as the kids, raising your voice and demanding that they quiet down. You simply, peacefully and calmly, move through the moment.

Before you know it, the kids may actually calm down themselves, having picked up your energy. Even if they do not, it will not matter. You have mastered the moment. You have changed the experience. Staying with this focus in the days and weeks which follow will show the children that becoming noisy is no longer a way of getting attention. In fact, they see just the opposite. This will produce a great awakening — in both you and your children.

The next thing that you will notice is that more
peacefulness prevails.

So will it be in every area of your life. Whatever
you choose to "be," its opposite number will appear
(or it will become more apparent that it was always
there!). Then, as you heal the illusion that this
"opposite" is who you are, and move with determined
focus into the continued and ever larger expression
of Who You *Really* Are, that which opposed you no
longer has any effect; you have rendered it null and
void.

And, as with all Masters, never again will you con-
demn that which others call evil, for you will know
that **what you resist persists**, and **what you look at
disappears**. That is, it ceases to hold its present
form, it ceases to produce its present effect.

And you will be surrounded by the darkness, yet
curse it not. And then you, as with all Masters, will
become a *Bringer of the Light*.

Recreating Step 5

Allow form to
create itself.

We come now finally to the question of Form. What form shall your service take? What will being a *Bringer of the Light* "look like"?

There are two ways to go about turning your heart's deepest desire into physical form. You may seek to make your desires fit into a predetermined form, or you may allow the form to create itself.

It is strongly suggested that the latter course be taken.

When we insist that our desires be made manifest in a particular form, we, in effect, limit God. Yet when we leave every option open, we make a space for marvelous creation.

One of the first questions asked by people who wish to serve others is, "What can I *do* to be a *Bringer of the Light?*" That should be the last question people ask.

Move first toward the State of Beingness in which a *Bringer of the Light* resides, then allow the "doingness" of your life to flow from that.

What is that State of Beingness? It is whatever you imagine it to be. You get to choose. You get to decide.

What is the Light you wish to share; that you wish to bring to, and call forth in, others? If you could give it a name, what would that be?

There is something burning inside of you which you know would, if ever fully released and fully expressed, make the lives of others better.

What is that? What does that *feel* like?

Remember, it is not something you would be *doing.* It is something you would be *being.*

Is it loving? Caring? Healing? You can be more of that *no matter what you are doing.*

Yet the magic of it is, the more of that you are

being, the more what you are *doing* will fall perfectly into place to allow you to "be" even more of that!

Trust this process. It works.

You will discover that forms — physical ways to "be" a thing — will suddenly start to just "show up."

Perhaps just one example here might make what we are trying to say a bit more clear.

A man once decided that he wanted to "be" the thing called "healing." This was a State of Being which he felt deeply within his soul, and he wished to express that.

Now he couldn't find a "job" out there in the so-called "real world" which allowed him to "do that." He looked in the want ads, but he didn't see many Help Wanted ads which said, "Major national corporation looking for healer," or, "Local company seeks healer for great entrance level position."

Discouraged, but undaunted, he decided to open his own business; start his own "practice." Still, he had no form, no mold, into which to pour the makings of his desire. So he created a form. He would be, he decided, a "crystal healer." Or maybe a "massage therapist." Or perhaps a "psycho-spiritual counselor." Or a "new age minister" for a church of his own devise.

He created a form which felt like it might work, and opened for business. And all was fine. Except hardly anyone came. And the few who did come didn't get the value, so left him with little or nothing. And he didn't feel "right" asking a fee, because, after all, he had just *made the whole game up*, quite *literally*, and he felt ashamed and embarrassed — if not to say, a bit guilty — to ask for or require what he felt he did not deserve.

So he starved to death. Not literally, of course. But figuratively, yes. His life by this time had turned to Jell-o. His partner left him, pronouncing him "crazy" as a result of this "midlife crisis" through which he was apparently moving. His old friends, too, thought he had flipped. And where once he had been really quite capable of taking care of himself, now he was living on the county, or taking government welfare in some other form, or, at best, barely eking by — but he was willing to make the sacrifice, because, after all, he was "doing what he wanted to do."

On his best days he could even *justify* the present state of his existence with that pronouncement. Still, something deep inside him told him there was a "lie" somewhere; an untruth. A formula he didn't know, a secret nobody told him. It shouldn't be this difficult to serve God or man, he told himself, sometimes bitterly. *It shouldn't be this hard.*

It isn't.

The secret is, *do not force the form.* Allow the Form to create itself.

This brings us to **Principle #5:**

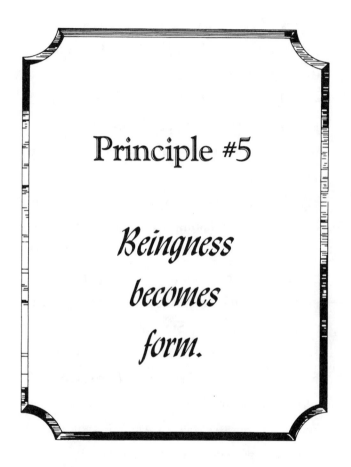

Principle #5

Beingness becomes form.

It is a fact of the Universe that you are a Being in formation. You do not need to bring any other "information" except *what you are* to the process of Life in order for What You Are to be made manifest in Form. You merely need to allow the process of "formation" to take place in its own way, in its own time.

And what is "its own way"? That is what this book has been explaining. Let's summarize it here.

The way Beingness becomes Form is, first, through self conception. That is, the Being conceives of what it wishes to "be" next **(Steps 1 & 2)**. It then moves into that State of Being immediately, regardless of external conditions or circumstances **(Step 3)**, or indeed, *in response to them* **(Step 4)**. Finally, it shapes itself around its own self concept, producing ways to experience *in form* that which it has been experiencing in formlessness.

Until all five steps are completed, you will find yourself uninformed. That is, you will not know Who You Are. You do not have enough in-formation. When *enough of You* is *in formation*, you will know and experience Who You Are *in physical form*.

This is another way of saying that your Outer Life will begin to reflect your Inner Reality about Who You Are, and Who You Choose to Be.

Remember, it all starts with a State of Being, which you choose independently. It can be quite an arbitrary choice; a State of Being you select simply because you prefer it or desire it. Yet that selection must be made before you can get anywhere.

So choose your life purpose, and let that life purpose be to achieve a state, or states, of "being." Then move into that State of Being no matter what. Watch as your body moves away from that which you are not. And do not resist that which opposes you. Simply stay centered in your Being by staying in the center *of* your Being, and watch the miracle.

Being *will produce* Form, sooner or later. It has no choice, for that is what Beingness *becomes*. It is the function of Beingess to produce Form. That is what God does. Or, more correctly, that is what God *is*.

God is Being; becoming Form.

And so are you.

So, there is nothing for you to *do*, actually. And the less done, the better.

Simply be.

Just...be.

Now, let's see if there is a way to apply this wisdom to the fictional man in our example, as we return to **Step 5.**

Let's say that this man did not spend any time or energy trying to put his Being into Form, but rather, allowed Form to create itself, *out* of his place of Being.

If he had done that, he would have simply moved *into* the place of Being in which he wished to reside, and remained there, stayed there, no matter *what* was going on — even if what was going on seemed to "oppose" what he wished to be. Perhaps especially so.

He would have simply *been* "healing" wherever he went to "work." He would have likewise been "healing" at home. At his church. With his friends. And whenever and wherever he could "be" that.

This is, in fact, what he did, soon after he abandoned his attempt to "make a living" doing what crystal healers do, or what massage therapists do, or what ministers do, or whatever he thought he had to do in order to "be" a "healer"...

In other words, instead of trying to be a HEALER, he decided to simply be HEALING.

He returned to what he had been "doing" before he'd decided to become a healer, which brought money back into his life almost instantly.

His wife returned to him, too, which was a source of great happiness to him. Even his health returned to normal, for it had been going slowly downhill during the months he'd been trying to "be" a "healer."

Now the problem was, how was he going to be able to tolerate his old occupation, knowing that what he really wanted to do was be a healer?

The answer was simple. He was going to see his

occupation in a new way. Just as he saw all of Life in a new way. For he now saw every moment and every situation as an opportunity to *be healing.* Being now on the road to life mastery, he saw *opposition as opportunity.*

This changed his whole life around. Where before at this job he saw conflict and wanted to run away from it, now he stood in the midst of it and brought healing. Within months his reputation as a healing, helping person spread. At work, he was soon removed from his former job and asked if he would accept a position in charge of employee morale. In his church, he became head of the team on Well Being. In his home, his spouse and his children found a new place of comfort to which to go in their moments of confusion, conflict, or despair.

Never before did this man have such a rich and wonderful experience of Who He Really Is.

But it went further. Soon, people in the community began to hear about him, mainly from his activities at church and on his job. One day he was asked by a friend if he would have the time and the willingness to volunteer with a local hospice organization. He knew instinctively this was a place where he could express and experience a part of himself, a side of himself, which longed for richer and richer unfoldment. His wife encouraged him. His minister thought it was a wonderful place for his skills. His employer even gave him a certain amount of time *on the clock* each month to undertake the work, if he would be kind enough to tell the hospice that he was representing the company. Soon, his work with the hospice became the company's "in-kind contribution" to this charitable organization.

The hospice staff saw his obvious desire, his ability, his enthusiasm for working with people — both patients and volunteers — in this unique setting. It took only a few months for the organization to realize that it had a very valuable man in its midst.

Then, as "luck" would have it, the head of Patient and Family Well Being at the hospice — a lay person working in close concert with the chief medical officer — moved to another town to accept a new opportunity...

You already know the end of this. Today, when he is not working directly with the terminally ill and their families in his home organization, this man travels the country speaking to hospice staff and volunteers. He has written a book, appeared on television, lectured at universities and churches all across America. Recently, at one of those lectures, he was introduced in a way which caught his ear.

"Ladies and gentlemen," the moderator began, "I would like to introduce to you a man who knows and deeply understands the meaning of the word 'healer'."

This is how it happens. Had this man tried to become a hospice advocate, author, and activist in the first place, he may never have succeeded. In fact, the idea of even *doing* this kind of thing may never had occurred to him.

Yet here he was. A Healer.

Doingness will follow Beingness, as surely as the night will follow the day. For Beingness cannot be denied, and never will. Yet Beingness knows its own reward. The man in our example knew himself as "healing" in his own experience long before he found himself "showing up" that way in the hospice setting.

Still, you may say, the example was fictional. Does it really work this way? Can you really "be who you are" and, out of that, make a life rather than a living?

I can only tell you this. There once was a man who wanted deeply to experience the part of himself called Wisdom, and Clarity.

It was an audacious desire, sweeping in its scope, almost blasphemous in its implications. Yet this is what he saw in himself. This is the part of God he saw within. And this is what he wished now to experience.

He looked and looked everywhere, yet he could not find a position, "Vice President in Charge of

Wisdom and Clarity."

He thought of creating his own firm, but no one was buying the concept.

So, he stopped trying to force his inner Beingness into an outer Doingness. He simply decided to just "be that," no matter what he was "doing."

To make money, he got into marketing and advertising. He did some writing. He became a radio talk show host.

Then one day, something unusual happened. He had a very interesting conversation with God...

The Steps and Principles
in this Book

Step 1: *Get clear about the purpose of your life.*
Principle #1:
Life is pointless, and that is God's Greatest Gift to us.

Step 2: *Translate your purpose from
Doingness to Beingness.*
Principle #2:
You are a Human Being, not a Human Doing.

Step 3: *Adopt right now the State of Being you
have described, no matter what you are doing.*
Principle #3:
*Everything you are being,
you are being because you choose to be.*

Step 4: *Observe Opposition and call it Opportunity.*
Principle #4:
*As soon as you decide Who and What you are, everything
unlike it will come into the space.*

Step 5: *Allow form to create itself.*
Principle #5:
Beingness becomes form.

A closing note:

Opportunities for more experiential work with the concepts and principles found in this book are available through the ReCreation Foundation created by Nancy and Neale Donald Walsch, principally through its 5-day intensive retreat, ReCreating Yourself, offered four times yearly, and facilitated by Neale.

Schedules for these spiritual retreats, attended by people from all over the world, are available from the Foundation upon request at 541-482-8806 or visit our website at www.conversationswithgod.org

ReCreation

*The Foundation for Personal Growth
and Spiritual Understanding*

PMB #1150
1257 Siskiyou Blvd.
Ashland, OR 97520
(541) 482-8806
Fax: (541) 482-6523
email: recreating@cwg.cc
website: http://www.conversationswithgod.org

Millennium Legacies, Inc., MLI,
publishes books, audio and video tapes, music CDs
and other materials agreeing with and advancing the
message of the *With God* series of books authored by
Neale Donald Walsch.

Our cost of writing, producing and distributing this book is approximately $3.25 per copy. Your price is $10. We provide this information in the interests of transparency.